Protein Powder Remixed: Delicious Snacks and Sweets Made Healthy with Protein Powder

Disclaimer and Terms of Use: Effort has been made to ensure that the information in this book is accurate and complete, however, the author and the publisher do not warrant the accuracy of the information, text and graphics contained within the book due to the rapidly changing nature of science, research, known and unknown facts and Internet. The Author and the publisher do not hold any responsibility for errors, omissions or contrary interpretation of the subject matter herein. This book is presented solely for motivational and informational purposes only.

Table of Contents

Ingredients:

- 1 C hemp protein powder
- ½ C cacao powder
- ¼ C arrowroot
- ¼ C coconut flour
- 1 tsp. baking soda
- 1 tsp. baking powder
- 1 egg
- 2 tsp. peppermint extract
- ½ C coconut nectar
- ½ C applesauce
- ½ C hot water

Directions:

I.   Add everything into a bowl and mix well, add the hot water last
II.   Spread runny batter into coconut-greased baking dish and bake for 30 minutes at 350 degrees.

Mint Chocolate Chip Protein Brownie Frosting

Ingredients:
- 1 avocado
- 1 ½ bananas
- ½ C coconut butter
- 6 T coconut oil
- 1 T vanilla extract
- 1 tsp. peppermint
- ½ C spinach
- 1 T water

Directions:

I.   Mix frosting ingredients and spread over cooled protein powder brownies

II.   Serve

Protein Pizza Crust

Ingredients:
- 1 ¼ C almond flour
- ¼ C protein powder
- 4 T husk powder
- ½ tsp. salt to taste
- 2 T parmesan cheese
- 1 T Italian seasoning
- 2 tsp. baking powder
- 2 eggs
- 1 C boiling water

Directions:

I. Set your oven to 375 degrees and combine all of your ingredients in a mixing bowl and stir well
II. Add ball of dough to baking sheet and roll out
III. Broil for about 7 - 8 minutes
IV. Add toppings and bake for another 6 – 10 minutes

Protein Pizza Recipes

Squash Pizza

Ingredients:
- 3 C mashed butternut squash
- pitted olives
- 1 C cherry tomatoes
- handful baby spinach
- mozzarella cheese

Directions:

Using the Protein Pizza Crust recipe above, add your toppings and follow the directions

Ingredients:

- 3 T olive oil
- 1/2 small red bell pepper, sliced
- 1/3 C broccoli, chopped
- 1/4 red onion, sliced
- 1/3 C Baby Bella mushrooms, sliced
- 1/4 C pesto sauce
- 1/2 C shredded mozzarella cheese
- 1 C crumbled goat cheese

Directions:

Prepare the Protein Pizza Crust per the recipe above and follow topping directions

Ingredients:
- olives
- anchovies
- 1 - 2 C mozzarella cheese
- mushroom pesto sauce

Directions:

Follow Protein Pizza Crust per the recipe but add ½ C diced mushrooms to crust

Zucchini Protein Pizza

Ingredients:
- Protein Pizza Crust
- 1 - 2 peeled and sliced zucchini
- pesto sauce
- mozzarella cheese

Directions:

Follow Protein Pizza Crust recipe and add toppings

Ingredients:
- 1 C soy milk
- 1 tsp. apple cider vinegar
- 1 C whole wheat flour
- 1/2 C protein plus
- 2 tsp. baking powder
- 1/2 tsp. baking soda
- 1/4 tsp. salt
- 1 tsp. cinnamon
- 1 tsp. vanilla extract
- 1/3 C canola oil
- 1/3 C sugar
- 1 1/2 C frozen blueberries

Directions:

I. Preheat oven to 375 degrees

II. Add your soy milk with vinegar and stir, set aside

III. Add all dry ingredients and open spot in the middle, add wet ingredients, everything but the berries, then fold in the berries

IV. Spray muffin tin and fill each tin about 2/3 full and bake for 20 - 25 minutes

V. Let cool and serve

Protein Pancakes

Ingredients:
- ½ C oats
- ½ C hot water
- 1 scoop protein powder
- ¼ C egg whites
- ¼ tsp. ground cinnamon

Directions:

I.   Mix oats and hot water and let sit a few minutes until light and fluffy

II.   Mix your protein powder with eggs and add oats, stirring lightly

III.   Stir in almond extract and cinnamon and use batter on griddle or skillet

IV.   Garnish with blueberries

Protein Powder Chocolate Pudding

Ingredients:
- 1 pkg. Jell-O instant pudding mixture
- 2 C nonfat milk
- 2 scoops protein powder

Directions:

I.   Mix everything together and let sit and chill for 10 minutes in fridge

II.   Serve

All Natural Protein Shakes

Ingredients:
- ¼ C cooking oats
- 1 ½ tsp. chia seeds
- 1 C coconut milk
- ¼ C greek yogurt
- 1 C pineapple chunks
- 2 tsp. sugar

Directions:

I.   Add everything to blender and blend to a smooth consistency
II.   Serve

Fruit Flax Smoothie

Ingredients:
- 1 C ice
- 1 C mixed berries
- ½ C oats
- 1 C milk
- ½ C Greek yogurt
- 2 T flax seeds

Directions:

I. Add ice and fruit to food processor and blend
II. Add oats and seeds and blend until smooth
III. Add yogurt and milk and pulse until creamy

Seaweed and Mint Protein Shake

Ingredients:
- 1 T Wakame Seaweed
- 2 T mint
- 2 frozen bananas
- 1 tsp. vanilla
- pinch spinach
- 1 C nut milk
- 2 t cacao

Directions:

I. Soak Seaweed for 10 minutes
II. Chop mint and spinach in blender
III. Add remaining ingredients and blend well
IV. Serve

Protein Apple Pie Smoothie

Ingredients:
- ½ C rolled oats
- ½ tsp. cinnamon
- ½ tsp. nutmeg
- 1 T almond butter
- ½ apple diced
- ½ C coconut milk
- 1 C ice
- ½ C water
- 1 - 3 T protein powder vanilla

Directions:

Add everything to blender and blend until smooth

Ginger Pear Protein Shake

Ingredients:
- 1 T ground flax
- 1 C water
- ½ T hemp seeds
- 2 T fresh ginger
- ¼ C almond milk
- ½ banana
- ½ pear
- 1 C spinach

Directions:

I. Add everything together and blend
II. Serve

Ingredients:
- 1/2 frozen banana
- 1/4 C walnuts
- 1 C almond milk
- 1 T cacao
- 1 tsp. vanilla
- 1/3 C frozen raspberries
- 1 T protein powder

Directions:

I.   Add everything together and blend
II.   Serve

Rooibos Protein Shake

Ingredients:
- 2 C green Rooibos
- 1 ½ C frozen blueberries
- 1 T flaxseed
- 1 T hemp seed
- ½ banana
- 2 T vanilla protein powder

Directions:

Combine everything and add to blender

Protein Cashew Smoothie

Ingredients:

- ¼ C cashews
- ½ banana, chopped
- 1 T cacao nibs
- ½ C ice
- ¼ C cold coffee
- 1 C almond milk
- ½ T coconut sugar
- 2 T protein powder

Directions:

Add everything together and blend until smooth

Strawberry Banana Smoothie

Ingredients:
- 1 pint strawberries
- 1 banana, chopped
- 1 C milk
- 1 serving yogurt
- 2 - 4 T protein powder

Directions:

I. Add everything in blender and blend until smooth
II. Serve once smooth

Protein Frosty Pumpkin

Ingredients:
- ½ banana
- 1 ½ frozen oranges
- 1 C coconut water
- 2 T pumpkin seeds
- 1 C baby spinach
- ¼ C protein powder

Directions:

Blend and serve

Almond Smoothie

Ingredients:
- 1 banana
- 1 ½ C frozen blueberries
- 1 T lemon juice
- 3 T almond butter
- 2 T flaxseed
- dates, pitted
- 2 C water

Directions:

Add everything and blend until smooth

Chamomile Smoothie

Ingredients:
- ½ C chamomile tea
- 1 T dried chamomile flowers
- 1 C almond milk
- ¼ C cooked quinoa
- ½ C strawberries
- 2 - 3 T protein powder, strawberry

Directions:

I.   Add flowers to hot water for about 5 minutes and strain
II.   Add remaining ingredients and blend
III.   Serve

The Blue Banana Smoothie

Ingredients:
- 2 ripe bananas
- 1 C frozen blueberries
- 2 T lemon juice
- 1 egg

Directions:

I.   Chop bananas and add to blender, blend until smooth
II. Serve

Banana Mango Smoothie

Ingredients:
- ¾ C Greek yogurt
- 2 C cubed mango
- 1 C ripe banana

Directions:

I.   Blend everything until smooth
II.   Serve

Avocado Shake

Ingredients:
- 1 C cold coconut water
- ¼ avocado
- 2 T sunflower seeds
- ½ bananas
- 1 T protein powder, chocolate

Directions:

Add everything to blender and blend until smooth

CPSIA information can be obtained at www.ICGtesting.com
Printed in the USA
LVOW06s2232170815

450539LV00014B/267/P